COMMON SENSE INVESTING WITH INDEX FUNDS

How to Build Wealth, Achieve Financial Freedom,
and Outperform Most Amateur and Professional
Investors Without Really Trying!

James Pattersenn Jr

www.theintelligentinvestorhub.com
www.howtoinvestinstocks.org

CONTENTS

Your Free Gift... 7

1 INTRODUCTION 8

2 START NOW!... 11

3 SHOW ME THE MONEY! 15

4 INVESTING INTELLIGENTLY 23

5 JOHN BOGLE: THE FATHER OF INDEX INVESTING 26

6 WHAT ARE INDEX FUNDS? 28

7 WHY IT MAKES COMMON SENSE TO INVEST IN INDEX FUNDS?............... 30

8 THE ADVANTAGES AND DISADVANTAGES OF INDEX FUNDS 34

9 USE DOLLAR COST AVERAGING TO CONTRIBUTE TO INVESTMENT FUNDS... 37

10 CONSTRUCTING A WINNING PORTFOLIO 40

11 POPULAR VANGUARD INDEX FUNDS 46

12 UNDERSTANDING THE MANAGEMENT EXPENSE RATIO (MER)............... 49

13 TYPES OF MUTUAL FUNDS... 52

14 MUTUAL FUND STRATEGIES 56

15 EXCHANGE-TRADED FUNDS (ETFS)... 60

16 TRACKING ERROR AND OTHER INVESTMENT TERMINOLOGY EXPLAINED ... 63

17 WHAT IF I'D LIKE TO DO IT ALONE? 67

18 CONCLUSION 69

Thank you so much for reading this book!.. 72

Your Free Gift.. 73

Acknowledgments 76

Customers Comments

I found this little book to be filled with useful information. I've been investing for several years, yet I found some things here that I can put into practice. I'd recommend this book to anyone who wants to learn how to invest their hard-earned money wisely.

Kristopher Rimmer

I found this to be an informative book and I learned new information. I recommend this book to those looking for more information on investing.

Kelly Pfister

This book is written so the amateur investor can easily understand investing concepts and strategies regarding Index Funds. The world of financial markets and investing is confusing to the average person, but this author wrote a short, easy to grasp book with information that I believe simplifies the big puzzle. Thank you Mr. Pattersenn.

William N. Weiss

As a complete novice to the world of investing, this did a wonderful job in breaking down and explaining investing and the value of certain index funds. It certainly makes the world of investment much less complicated!

Jacob Hobbs

This is a FABULOUS introductory text on Index Funds and how to handle those sorts of investments. I learned a lot and even a few new things about investing overall. Highly recommended if that's what you're looking for. Two thumbs up!

Mrs. Whatsit

This book contains valuable information that was easy to understand. It was a quick read, and I didn't feel the information was too overwhelming (i.e. crammed into too few pages).

Chelsea Falin

This book is a great investment guide for investors who are looking to learn how to use index funds to build wealth while achieving financial freedom. If you are an investor who is interested in building wealth and achieving financial freedom without the complex strategies of day trading, swing trading, and other stock trading systems. Then this book is for you and I will recommend it to anyone who is an investor.

Minnie10

DISCLAIMER

This book was published for educational purposes, and it's not intended to provide specific personalized advice. It's sold with the understanding that the author or publisher is not engaged in rendering legal, accounting, investment or other professional services. Investing in stocks and the stock market involves varying degrees of risk, and there's no assurance that a specific stock, investment principle or investment strategy will be profitable for an individual, group or organization. All information contained in this book was gathered from sources believed to be reliable, but neither the author nor the publisher can accept responsibility for its accuracy.

The author or publisher specifically denies any responsibility for liability, loss, or risk, professional or otherwise, which is incurred as a consequence, directly or indirectly, of the use and application of any of the contents of this book.

ISBN 987-0-9895464-8-5 (Softcover)

Your Free Gift

As a way of showing my appreciation, I want to send you my FREE

REPORT,

5 Highly-Rated ETFs That Can Make You Rich.

Contained within this report are:

- ETFs that have easily outperformed the overall stock market over the last decade and beyond!
- ETFs that are highly-rated by professional investment analysts!
- ETFs that offer high return opportunities and are excellent long-term plays!
- ETFs that hold some of the best and most financially sound companies in the world.
- ETFs that are predicted to deliver big returns well beyond the pandemic!

Please enter your email at the link below and I will send you a copy of

this Free Report:

https://mailchi.mp/30fb211f84c6/common-sense-investing-with-index-funds

1

INTRODUCTION

W hen I first began my in-depth research into investing more than a decade ago, it was estimated that seventy percent of the professional money managers which included: mutual funds, investment banks, brokerage firms, and hedge funds, failed to beat the stock market over the long-term. Today, that estimate has climbed above ninety percent. Can you imagine? Ninety percent of the pros that we entrust our money to in hopes of receiving a satisfactory return, fail to beat the market, yet the stock market is absolutely one of the best places, if not the best, for us normal folks to invest and build wealth, to achieve financial freedom.

In a March 2013 article published in *USA Today,* author Al Neuharth summed things up nicely by stating, -Most of us hope to get richer as life goes on. All of us should realize that the surest way to do that is by smart and regular investments in the stock market.ll In this guide, when I talk about investing in the stock market, I'm talking specifically about investing in index funds. I want to let you in on a little secret. You don't need to beat the market! If you buy the market, you're going to beat most other investors out there, and you're going to build wealth while doing so.

I consider myself a very good stock picker when it comes to buying individual stocks, but I also realize that this type of investing isn't for everyone. It takes time for an individual to develop the skills needed to successfully pick individual stocks. I know! I have been doing so for more than a decade.

Some people, no doubt, would like to keep things much simpler when it comes to investing, and yet gain their financial independence. That's where index funds come in. Index funds are great wealth builders, yet they allow the investor the opportunity to simplify the investment process. Although I'm a stock picker at heart, I still love index funds and actually hold some in my own investment portfolios.

Here's what Warren Buffett, known as the -world's greatest investor,‖ said on CNBC's *On The Money,* -Consistently buy an S&P 500 low-cost index fund.‖ He went on to say, -I think it's the thing that makes the most sense practically all of the time.‖ If the world's greatest investor believes this, then he sees index funds as great long-term wealth builders. According to Buffett, $10,000 invested in an index fund back in 1942, would be worth $51 million today. If index funds are good enough for Mr. Buffett, they certainly ought to be good enough for us. That's just Common Sense Investing!

Finally, I wanted to mention that if you have read some of my other books, you may notice that I have included several chapters or sections directly from those books. My purpose in doing so was not to use that information as fillers to make this book longer, because I could have easily written a much longer book without including that information. I included chapters or sections from my other books that I felt were important and relevant to readers of this book also. Whether you are investing in individual stocks, mutual funds, or index funds, some things are applicable to them all. So, it is my hope that you enjoy the information presented herein.

2

START NOW!

T hroughout my childhood I was never taught much, neither at home or school, when it came to budgeting, managing my finances, or investing. In those days, Americans in general were taught to get a good job, work hard, and save money; and that by doing so, everything should work out alright in retirement. Well, when I look at our elderly population today, things have not worked out for the majority of them when it comes to their finances. Most are struggling and still living from check to check, except instead of it being a paycheck, it's usually a Social Security check. Now, there's nothing wrong with receiving a Social Security check. As a matter of fact, I look forward to the day, if God permits, when I will begin receiving one myself. That is, if the government can get its act together concerning Social Security and the insanely high national deficit that we carry as a nation.

The mistake that Americans have made, is in their failure to save and invest enough money in preparation for their retirement; and it seems that our youth population is making the same mistake. Our youths are much smarter than my generation and all the generations that have preceded them, except in the area of their finances and investing. When I consider today's youths, it is easy to see that they have so many advantages in comparison to previous generations.

For example, it's much easier for most to graduate with a high school diploma, when compared to most of the generations that preceded them that were only allowed to attend school during inclement weather. It's true! There was a time in our history when children were required to stay home and work the farm instead of attending school. I know because I have spoken with many of those senior citizens, and many of them cannot read. When the weather was good, they had to farm or work other laborious jobs to help the family. Literally, they had to work to eat.

The youths of today would hardly find themselves in such harsh circumstances; yet, many of our youth are still dropping out of school when a good education is more important now, than it has ever been. Our government has created an assortment of programs and incentives to encourage our youth to attend and to stay in school, and yet more than 1.2 million students drop out of high school every year here in the United States.

So, I speak directly to all of America's youth that may be reading this guide, and I encourage you to take some of those financial and investing courses offered at your schools. Join that investment club that you have been curious about. Talk to those instructors, professors, and teachers overseeing those programs and courses and learn from them everything that you can, while you are still young.

If you would learn to sacrifice now when it comes to all of those material things that don't last and start investing today, there's absolutely no reason why the majority of you could not obtain financial security and wealth in your 40s or sooner, and that's a fact.

Bernard Kelly, the author of *Flipping Burgers to Flipping Millions* is the perfect example of what our youth can achieve at a very young age. After graduating from high school, he went straight to work for McDonald's cooking fries and by the age of 30, he was a millionaire. Amazingly, he achieved this by working only at McDonald's and by investing only income that he earned at McDonald's. Our youth can achieve amazing things, if we encourage them and let them know that they can do it!

I now speak directly to the older generations of adults that are headed toward retirement within the next decade or sooner, but have not saved or have not sufficiently saved enough for retirement. It's important that you get started now. Don't wait another day! Depending on your circumstances, you can still build a sizeable nest egg that will assist you in your retirement years. It's all about the power of compounding.

The reinvesting of all income that's earned from investing, results in your money growing. This growth is known as compound growth. Compound growth is what allows an investor to take a small sum of money and, in time, become extremely wealthy. It has been called the -Eighth Wonder of the World.‖ All great investors relied or rely on the power of compounding to grow their wealth and so should you. It doesn't take a lot of money for you to achieve great wealth. It's just important that you get started investing now and let the power of compounding work for you.

3

SHOW ME THE MONEY!

Most people who think they don't have the money they need to start investing, usually actually do. The situation simply boils down to being smarter with the income they presently earn. When we begin to take a serious look at the situation, most of us have areas in which we are wasting money. This wasted money could instead be used to put us on a path to a financially secure future.

Here are some ideas or suggestions on where to find that extra money to start your investment program.

1. Participate in your employer's sponsored retirement plan such as: the 401(k), 403(b), or SEP (Simplified Employee Pensionplan).

By contributing as little as 5% of your gross pay into your retirement plan, you are on your way to building a serious nest egg and at the same time, you will reduce your taxable income. In no time at all, you will not even miss the contributions and will simply adapt to living on a little less income. In addition, your employer will usually match a percentage of your contributions, which actually gives you free money to invest and grow your wealth.

2. Invest your next pay raise.

When you receive your next pay raise, do not start spending it. Start investing it consistently, and act as if it was never received.

3. Invest your next bonus.

Treat your next bonus as you would your next pay raise and invest it, instead of spending it.

4. Invest your next tax refund.

Treat it as you would your next pay raise or bonus, as previously mentioned.

5. Increase your withholding allowances to bring home more money now.

If you find yourself receiving a large tax refund every year, you may be paying too much in income taxes throughout the year. A much better option would be to have less money withheld for taxes, by increasing your withholding allowances. Most personnel departments can usually assist an employee with figuring out the correct amount of withholding allowances to carry. It's very important to compute the correct withholding allowances, because you do not want to be stuck with a big tax bill when filing your income tax return.

6. Consolidate high-interest debts.

Consolidate high-interest loans and credit cards into a single loan with a low interest rate. Doing so should get you out of debt quicker and save you money in interest charges, too.

7. Pay off higher interest loans first.

If you are unable to or just do not want to consolidate your debt, concentrate your efforts into paying off higher interest loans first.

8. Make good use of earmarked money.

Once you have paid off a debt, do not start spending the additional money that becomes available. Take the extra income and use it to pay off other debts, to invest wisely.

9. Reduce the amount that you pay for prescription drugs.

If you or your family members are required to take prescription drugs, always ask for generics if they are available, but be sure to consult with your physician first. Generic drugs must meet the same strict federal guidelines as name brand drugs and work just as well.

10. Buy straight term life insurance.

You don't need all the bells and whistles when it comes to life insurance. The main purposes of life insurance are to replace lost income and to pay off debts. When it comes to value and savings, a straight term life insurance policy is hard to beat.

11. Do not smoke or drink.

Both are very expensive and unhealthy habits that will cost you both now and later, in terms of money and health. If you refuse to quit, at the very least, cut back drastically on these bad habits.

12. Do not purchase credit Life and disability insurance offered to you by the lending institutions.

This type of insurance is offered to individuals by banks and other financial institutions when they apply for a loan. It's supposed to pay the loan off if the borrower becomes disabled or dies. This type of insurance is not necessary, and the lenders cannot base their loan decisions on whether or not you purchase it. It's simply another way for financial institutions to make money since they rarely have to pay claims on this type of insurance.

13. Do not carry large life insurance policies on small children.

Never carry large life insurance policies on small children. Remember, life insurance's main purposes are to replace lost income and to pay off existing debts.

14. Purchase auto insurance and homeowners insurance at cheaper rates than you are currently paying.

When it comes to auto and homeowners insurance, the cost varies among different agencies. Shopping around could result in savings of several hundred dollars annually in premiums.

15. Increase the deductible on your auto and homeowners insurance.

Increasing the deductible on your auto and homeowners insurance could result in savings of 20-30% in annual premiums.

16. Consider dropping collision and comprehensive coverage on older vehicles.

When a vehicle is worth only a few thousand dollars, consider dropping the collision and comprehensive coverage. Many people actually pay more in annual premiums than their vehicles are worth. It just does not make sense to do that.

17. Drive a fuel-efficient vehicle.

If you have more than one vehicle, drive the one that gets the best fuel efficiency. If you are considering buying a vehicle, purchase a certified used vehicle that gets good fuel efficiency.

18. Do not buy a new vehicle every few years.

If no major problems exist with your vehicle, get good use from it before committing to a new one, and the payments that come along with it.

19. Cut up all credit cards except one.

Start paying cash for everything. You will find that when you pay cash for everything, you will be less inclined to spend your hard-earned money or to waste it on items that you do not need. Using several credit cards will keep you in debt forever. Cut up all credit cards except one, and use it only for true emergencies such as an auto repair bill or an insurance deductible.

20. Get rid of unnecessary bank and credit card fees.

If you pay annual fees for your credit card, switch to a low interest card that charges no fees. If you're also paying banking fees, rid yourself of them by talking with the bank's management and requesting that the fees be waived or lowered.

21. Stay away from ATM machines.

Get rid of the ATM cards and debit cards or use them as little as possible. ATM cards and debit cards make it too easy and convenient to access and spend your hard-earned money.

22. Carry your lunch to work.

Carry your lunch and other snacks to work. Doing so can easily result in savings of several hundred dollars annually.

23. Do not eat out.

If you are going to eat out, do so only on special occasions. A night out with the family could easily cost you more than a hundred bucks, so prepare and eat your meals at home.

24. Do not play the lottery.

Playing the lottery is like flushing money down the toilet. You will never see it again. Put your money into an excellent selection of stocks, mutual funds or index funds instead.

25. Get rid of unnecessary phone services.

If you find yourself with costly phone services that you do not use, get rid of them. It's a known fact that phone companies push extra services on the consumer, knowing the services will hardly be used. Phone companies love it when you purchase those services since they cost them very little, but bring in large profits. If you use a cell phone, be sure to sign up for a calling plan that has excellent terms, such as free minutes and low monthly payments.

26. Cancel cable or satellite television.

Get rid of the expensive cable or satellite television that continues to increase in cost year after year. Install a good digital antenna that provides you with several local and regional channels to view. If you insist on keeping your service, get rid of everything except the basic package.

27. Rent movies or join a video rental club.

Rent movies instead of going to the movie theater. If you think that the admission is expensive, just wait until you pay for the popcorn and drinks.

28. Look for forms of free entertainment for the family.

Most towns, cities and counties sponsor free forms of entertainment for the entire family. Check with your city and county government to see what free events are scheduled. These activities can be both fun and educational.

29. Get rid of the mini warehouse.

Make room at home to store your items or hold a large garage sale. Many times, the annual expense of renting the mini warehouse cost more than the items being stored are worth.

30. Drop the fitness center membership if it's not being used.

If you have not used the fitness center within the last year, then you probably won't. Find creative ways to exercise at home.

31. Conserve energy.

Make your home more energy efficient by properly insulating the attic, installing a programmable thermostat, using energy efficient light bulbs and talking with your local utility service provider for recommendations on how to conserve energy. When you conserve energy, you save money.

32. Getapart-timejob.

If necessary, find part-time work and use the income from it to start your investment program.

These are a few simple and effective ways of finding extra money to invest. These are areas we take for granted and most of the time we don't even realize how much money we really are wasting. Implementing some of these recommendations could easily uncover several thousand dollars in real money, for investing. The individual with the millionaire's mindset is the one who's willing to sacrifice now, in exchange for future wealth.

4

INVESTING INTELLIGENTLY

I t's amazing how the tables have turned. Gary Kaminsky, author and successful Wall Street money manager, stated in his book *Smarter than the Street,* -Taking personal control of your financial future makes more sense now than ever before.‖ Additionally, he stated, -Research shows that in the last two plus decades, the percentage of money managers that beat the S&P 500 is down by a significant margin over the percentage for the decades prior to 1987.‖

Index funds, mutual funds, hedge funds and other investment funds are the pooling of money from several individuals and/or organizations into stocks, bonds, money market instruments and a variety of other types of equities, with the goal of earning a profit. The funds raise money for investment purposes from the issuance of fund shares. The individuals or teams managing those funds are experts in their fields, that use very powerful and sometimes complex investment tools to assist them with investment decisions. Yet, most funds still fail to outperform the overall stock market (stock market index). If that's the case, then it would seem that the small investor does not stand a chance of investing successfully in the stock market, however that belief could not be further from the truth.

So, why do most fund and other money managers fail so badly at their job? The answer is, most managers exert too much effort and energy into constantly investing in the hottest stocks at the moment. This is done in hopes of obtaining a quick, large profit from the investment. Along with this investment strategy comes an increased exposure to risk, because what's usually hot today won't be hot tomorrow! The small investor or individual investor must think long-term if he or she is going to achieve excellent returns from investing in the stock market. Short-term investing is just too risky. Although the stock market can be very volatile and unpredictable in the short-term, it's much more predictable over the long term.

The intelligent investor should purchase index funds or individual stocks with the intention of holding them no fewer than 10 years. In doing so, exposure to risk is decreased and personal feelings and emotions are kept out of the market, allowing him or her to be positioned for excellent future investment returns. It's also very important to take a nontraditional approach to investing. Don't do what everybody else is doing, and don't buy or sell because everybody else is doing so. If you and I fall into the trap of doing what everyone else is doing, it's almost guaranteed that the performance of our investment portfolios will be just like everyone else.

The most successful investors have been those that run to the stock market when everyone else is running from it. They buy when everyone else is selling and sell when everyone else is buying. They are happiest when the stock market has been beaten down, when there's a big market correction or when panic selling is present within the market. They know that it's at those times when equities, can usually be purchased at a serious discount to their intrinsic or fair value.

Remember, when pessimism is at its greatest, the most opportune times present themselves for making a lot of money, by investing in the stock market. In his book *Common Stocks and Uncommon Profits,* Philip A. Fisher states, -The wise investor can profit if he can think independently of the crowd and reach the right answer, when the majority of financial opinion is leaning the other way.‖ I found that all of the great investors were unique and nontraditional in their approach to investing. They simply refused to follow the crowd and you and I should do the same thing.

5

JOHNBOGLE:
THE FATHER OF INDEXINVESTING

John Bogle, commonly referred to as Jack, is known as *The Father of Index Investing* and *The Father of Index Funds*. Bogle was born in Montclair, New Jersey on May 8, 1929. He attended Princeton University and graduated magna cum laude in 1951, with a degree in Economics. While at the university, he began to develop his philosophies and theories on investing and believed that investors could win and build real wealth by matching the performance of an index, such as the S& P 500.

After graduation, Bogle went to work for Wellington Management from 1951 to 1974, but was fired because of a merger decision he made. In 1974, he found the Vanguard Group Inc., and in 1976 he introduced the first retail index fund known as the Vanguard 500. At Vanguard, Bogle stressed the importance of placing the investors' interest first and held to his belief that low-cost index investing was the answer. More than four decades later, the Vanguard 500 index fund is still going strong and throughout most of that period, it has easily outperformed the majority of actively managed mutual funds.

Although Bogle was initially mocked for his introduction of the index fund to the market, he proved to be a true visionary and was even named as one of the -World's 100 Most Powerful and Influential Peoplell by Time Magazine in 2004. From those early days of mockery, it seems that Bogle has proven that he was right in his beliefs on index investing; since index funds have consistently provided superior performance, compared to most actively managed funds.

Vanguard has grown to become one of the world's largest investment management companies, with more than five trillion in global assets under management. Although Mr. Bogle died in January of 2019, his philosophy of index investing will remain a force to be reckoned with for a long time to come. Perhaps, even he did not realize the enormous impact and influence he would have on the investment world. After all, it was him that gave us little guys and gals a fighting chance against the large and powerful investment institutions. Even more, it's a fight that we can win!

6

WHAT ARE INDEX FUNDS?

Warren Buffett, considered by many to be the greatest investor in stock market history, stated, "investors should know their limits." There's clear wisdom in this statement that relates to everyday life, and it's knowing what you can and can't do. In other words, it's about knowing your limitations when it comes to specific situations or circumstances.

Ask yourself, would you fight a grizzly bear if you had the opportunity to do so? You would probably say that's crazy since the bear is very large and powerful and you're probably going to be killed? Okay, it's an extreme example, but you get the picture. You realize that you can't fight with a grizzly bear and win. Well, in the stock market, sometimes it's the same, and yes, there are people on Wall Street and Main Street who fight bears and bulls with a great equalizer every day. That equalizer is known as the index fund, which provides investors with the resources they need to surpass their constraints. In other words, they grant investors the ability to fight with the grizzly bear…and win! Here's a definition for index fund:

An index fund is a type of mutual fund with a portfolio constructed to match or track the components of a financial market index, such as the Standard & Poor's 500 Index (S&P 500).

Most index funds are greatly diversified and represent investment options in a portfolio that could only be matched by a small number of investors. Because they have such a large portion of the market in their portfolios, that makes it very hard to outperform index funds over the long-term and few investors are capable of outpacing the long-term performance of major indices (indexes) such as the Dow, the S&P 500, or the Nasdaq.

7

WHY IT MAKES COMMON SENSE
TO INVEST IN INDEX FUNDS?

Reason #1: Index funds outperform the vast majority of actively managed funds. Two-thirds of actively managed mutual funds have failed to beat their relevant index in a typical year, and over 80 percent (I believe an accurate estimate is over 90 percent) have been unable to outperform their relevant index over a 20-year period.

Actively managed funds, where a director or board makes the investment decisions and expect extraordinary success, fail to deliver it due to numerous crippling costs. Morningstar data shows that operational, investment and opportunity costs for the average actively managed mutual fund result in total annual expenses of more than 2.5 percent. Index funds, on the other hand, reduce costs by using computer systems instead of expensive financial experts, and by trading far less regularly than active funds. A typical index fund has a total annual expense of less than 0.5%.

Therefore, the average index investor outperforms the average active investor by 2 percent annually, based on the numbers above. Let's consider the indexing advantage, although 2 percent doesn't sound like much. Assuming an initial $10,000 investment and an average market return of 8 percent, an index investor will retire with a total account value of $372,000, while an active investor will retire with just $145,000–that's less thanhalf!

Reason #2: Investing in index funds provides simplicity and transparency to an investment portfolio. Individual investors pay unprecedented attention to their investment portfolios in the wake of the recent financial crisis. Some abandon high-priced professionals and manage their own money; others look with increased scrutiny and skepticism at the activities of their advisor. It is challenging to invest effectively, but it doesn't have to be complex.

According to a report by Ibbotson and Associates, the asset allocation or the percentages of various types of financial assets (e.g., shares, bonds, cash) in an investor's portfolio can be attributed to more than 90 percent of investment returns. Unfortunately, when working with a portfolio of actively managed funds, asset allocation can be difficult to determine. In the hope of increasing returns, active managers can drift from their described investment style (known as *style drift*), so an active-managed "small-cap value fund", could consist of some large-cap, growth, or cash holdings at any time. Style drift can potentially reduce overall portfolio diversification, which may result in increased investment risks.

By contrast, an index investor's asset allocation is greatly simplified. A small-cap value index fund always keeps a 100% investment in small-cap value stocks, so the investor knows precisely what he is getting for each dollar invested. This secrecy vastly simplifies the task of managing portfolios. When market movements make the portfolio too risky or conservative, management will rebalance the positions within the portfolio, to restore the portfolio to its correct asset allocation.

Reason #3: Investing in index funds serves to counteract several harmful biases in behavior. You are your worst enemy when it comes to investing! Overconfidence, aversion to loss, and herding are just some of the natural human tendencies that can prevent you from making the right investment decisions. When paired with a strict rebalancing plan, a risk-appropriate index portfolio provides a dominant defense against these adverse behavioral powers. Over time, your portfolio will deviate from your targeted asset allocation. For example, your original asset allocation target may have been 80% stocks and 20% bonds, but because of fluctuations in the market, your asset allocation is now 60% stocks and 40% bonds. Rebalancing is simply the process of bringing your asset allocation in line with your original target. In this example, you would sell 20% of your bonds and that amount to your stock positions.

We (people) tend to be overconfident about our physical and mental abilities. Eight out of 10 college students think they're better-than-average drivers, and seven out of 10 Americans believe they are smarter than the average American. They also appear to be unwilling to suffer defeat. This phenomenon makes us feel more pain from a loss of $1,000 than happiness from a gain of $1,000. As a result, we tend to hold on to losing investments (to avoid the pain associated with realizing the loss) and sell too soon when it comes to winning investments. Both of these practices are destroyers of wealth.

You may consistently eliminate these negative behavioral biases by creating a risk-appropriate portfolio and preserving it through a rebalancing plan. Second, reduce the harmful effects of overconfidence by building a portfolio based on your risk potential, not based on what you feel will be achieved by the economy or a specific sector. Next, fight your tendency to be opposed to losing by setting portfolio rebalancing targets, thereby eliminating your ability to make adverse purchase/sell decisions. Last but not least, ignore the herd and follow your plan!

By investing in a risk-appropriate index fund portfolio, you can increase your return on your investment, simplify the portfolio management process, and counter the harmful prejudices that are naturally present in your psyche. The advantages of index investing make this approach boring, but it has been said by great investor and speculator George Soros, -If you're having fun, you're probably not making any money.ll

8

THE ADVANTAGES AND DISADVANTAGES OF INDEX FUNDS

F or most investors, consistently investing in index funds is probably one of the most intelligent investment decisions that they could make, when we consider the fact that index funds commonly outperform most actively managed funds types. While some actively managed funds will outperform their benchmark index in any given year, it's very rare for them to accomplish that feat in subsequent years. Now, let's look at some of the advantages offered through the ownership of indexfunds.

Advantage # 1: Index funds are extremely tax efficient, since they have very low turnover rates. The turnover rate is the percentage of a fund's holdings that are exchanged (sold and replaced) in a given year. When funds sell positions within their portfolios from which they have received capital gains, taxes must be paid on those capital gains in the tax year for which those capital gains were received. Since index funds rarely sell or make changes to their holdings, they pay very little taxes on capital gains. With all else being equal, funds with higher turnover rates will pay more in taxes than funds with lower turnover rates.

Advantage #2: Since index funds are passive investments, they incur much lower expenses to manage. Actively managed funds charge much higher fees that may be the result of research by analyst, transaction fees, bonuses, and numerous other fees or expenses which simply are non-existent with index funds. This equates to a better performance of index funds when compared to the performance of actively managed funds.

Advantage #3: Index funds provide lower risks because of the instant diversification that they provide. For instance, an index fund that mimics the S&P 500 contains the same 500 companies as the S&P 500. When investors own index funds such as the Vanguard S&P 500, their investment risks are reduced because of the high level of diversification that's provided by the fund. A few bad apples are not going to have much of an impact on the fund's overall performance.

Although index funds have proven themselves to be excellent investments, as with other types of investments, there are a few minor disadvantages to owning index funds. Let's look at them next.

Disadvantage #1: When you invest in an invest index fund, you will not outperform its benchmark index. Since index funds are designed to mimic their benchmark, that's to be expected. I disagree with both professionals and nonprofessionals that say investors that invest in index funds only receive average returns. It's simply not true. Investors that stick with a discipline, long-term plan of index investing will receive returns that are much higher than average. Remember, more than 90 percent of actively managed funds fail to outperform index funds. That 90 percent is the average group that obtains those average returns.

Disadvantage #2: Index funds are rigid investments, meaning that they lack flexibility. When the stock market tumbles and rolls, the managers of index funds must let their funds tumble and roll with the market. In other words, the managers' hands are tied. Although this fact is listed as a disadvantage, I think that it's a good thing since investors tend to be their own worst enemies when it comes to investing. What I mean is that the poor returns that the majority of investors obtain are usually the result of something that the investors did or didn't do. Greed and emotions are usually the culprits that influence the decisions that are made by the majority of individual investors...and many professional investors. Yes, even professional investors.

As far as I'm concerned, the advantages for investing in and owning index funds far outweigh the disadvantages of not doing so. After all, index funds have the performance history to back them up. The fact that index funds have consistently outperformed most active investors, regardless of whether they were amateur investors or professional money managers, proves that index funds are great investments that each investor should consider owning in his or her portfolio.

9

USE DOLLAR COST AVERAGING TO CONTRIBUTE TO INVESTMENT FUNDS

The question has been asked again and again about the best strategy or method to use when adding a new stock position to an investment portfolio. Some professionals believe that the entire sum of money to be invested should be spent all at once for the purchase. In other words, some believe in a one-time lump sum purchase. Other professionals believe that an investor should gradually build a position for each new investment through a program of dollar cost averaging or by splitting the purchases up. Here's a definition of dollar cost averaging:

The process of investing a fixed amount or percentage of money into an investment at regular intervals regardless of the investment's cost.

According to research, lump sum investing will usually produce a higher return than dollar cost averaging about 7 times out of 10. The drawback to investing a lump sum into a particular investment is that the investment could experience a significant drop in price soon after its purchase. I must admit that I'm no stranger to such an event happening to me on several occasions. Let me tell you about just one of my experiences.

Many years ago, I spent a lump sum of more than $5000 buying shares of First Marblehead Corporation, only to watch the stock tumble in price, turning my investment into less than $2000 in only a few weeks. In the end, I lost most of my money on that investment. Had I split my purchases up over a few months or weeks, I would have become suspicious of the sudden drop in my shares' price and would have at the very least reassessed the situation and my reason for purchasing First Marblehead. I also would have held off purchasing more shares of the stock, until I had a better picture of what was going on with the company; and more than likely would have only lost about one-third of the money that I lost. I eventually drew the conclusion that First Marblehead was a financial stock that got crushed along with all other financial stocks during the brutal 2008-2009 period of the Great Recession. In the end, the business never recovered and was taken private. Fortunately for me, I held the stock long enough to offset the loss with capital gains from some other investments. So, I don't mind telling you that I'm not a big fan of the strategy of investing a lump sum into a stock or any other security sold in the market.

Dollar cost averaging, unlike investing a lump sum, reduces the risk of investing a large amount of money into an investment at the wrong time, and through its use, an investor will buy more shares at lower prices and fewer shares when prices are higher. There has been a considerable amount of controversy concerning dollar cost averaging, but I believe that it is especially useful for employees that invest through 401Ks and other types of employer-sponsored retirement plans. Once the retirement account is set up, the employer deducts contributions from the employee's check during each pay period, which makes the process automatic and easier for even the undisciplined saver to build wealth.

Another advantage to dollar cost averaging is the fact that it allows an individual to invest small sums of money into the stock market, since most individuals probably don't have lump sums of money to invest. In time, the investor that sticks to a steady plan of dollar cost averaging, is likely to have a substantial nest egg when the time comes to retire.

10

CONSTRUCTING A WINNINGPORTFOLIO

F irst, I want to mention that neither I, nor the publisher, is receiving any type of compensation for mentioning Vanguard in this book, nor are we affiliated with Vanguard in any way. I mention or use Vanguard throughout this book because I think that it's a great company that offers great funds. Vanguard isn't trying to be like other companies, other companies are now trying to be like Vanguard. There are other very good mutual fund companies out there, and it's up to you to determine which one is best for you

There are strategies that can be used to create a successful investment portfolio that is easy to manage. My aim here is to share a fundamental investment strategy that can be used by anyone. Your first step is to open a brokerage account, ideally, one that can also give you the option of setting up an Individual Retirement Account (IRA). Keep in mind that using an IRA account allows you to make tax deferred contributions. This strategy can be used to build a sizeable retirement nest egg or to put you on the path to financial freedom.

This strategy can also be used for an investment account from which you plan to make withdrawals whenever you want, without the restrictions that are typically imposed on IRA accounts.

Investing in index funds such as the Dow, S&P 500, domestic and international stock markets, and even the overall bond market is your next step. The index fund replicating the S&P 500, for example, would carry the same stocks at the same weight as the S&P 500. So why invest in an S&P 500 index fund? The S&P 500 is known as an economic indicator tracking the performance of the United States ' largest 500 publicly traded firms. Most financial professionals evaluate their performance against the S&P 500's results. On average, the S&P 500's performance will outperform most professional investors' returns in any given year.

By investing in an index fund such the S&P 500, you are setting yourself up to earn market returns (above average returns) on your investment. Index funds have lower expense ratios and the lower the cost of your investments, the higher the likely returns. With an expense ratio as low as 0.04%, index funds are desirable compared to regular mutual funds with expense ratios ranging from 0.50% to 1.5%. A percentage difference may seem trivial, but long-term spending can add up to thousands of dollars.

You may now be wondering about where to find these investment vehicles. Vanguard provides the right choices, as do many other investment firms that are specifically designed to track shares, securities, municipal bonds, industries, and sectors. For example, you can invest in index funds designed to track several sectors such as technology, real estate, energy, etc. Here are three good fund options that Vanguard offers for building a winning portfolio.

Vanguard 500 Index Fund Admiral Shares (VFIAX) follows the S&P 500 with an expense ratio of 0.04%.

Vanguard Total Bond Market Index Fund Admiral Shares (VBTLX) provides wide exposure to U.S. investment grade bonds and has an expense ratio of 0.05%.

Vanguard International Value Investor Shares (VTRIX) provides international exposure to your portfolio and has an expense ratio of 0.38%. You can also find index funds that track stock markets in Europe and Asia.

These are just a few of Vanguard's many fund options. You can choose to spread your portfolio across these three different index funds in a range of mixed proportions, depending on your age and risk tolerance. Of course, it is up to you to perform your own research to determine which investment option or options are best for you.

Here are a few asset allocation models to consider:

High Risk(Young)

60% in Vanguard 500 Index Fund

25% in Vanguard International Value Fund

15% in Vanguard Total Bond Market Index Fund

Medium Risk (Mid-Life)

50% in Vanguard 500 Index Fund

15% in Vanguard International Value Fund

35% in Vanguard Total Bond Market Index Fund

Low Risk(Older)

20% in Vanguard 500 Index Fund

5% in Vanguard International Value Fund

75% in Vanguard Total Bond Market Index Fund

Your allocation percentage will probably shift with the passing of time and market fluctuations, when one index fund performs better or worse than the other two index funds within your portfolio. It is, therefore, essential to rebalance your portfolio to bring your allocation levels into line with your risk tolerance; this also limits over-exposure to one class over the other.

I think you should know that there are many different types of index funds available for the investor that can add to the diversification of his or her portfolio. I will not list them here, because there are far too many, but what I will do is list some of the more popular index fund types for you. The list follows next:

Different Types of Index Funds

Broad-based Index Funds- These funds are designed to track the performance of an entire market or a subset of the market. Examples are the Vanguard Total Stock Market Index Fund (VTSMX) and the Vanguard Total Bond Market Index Fund (VBTLX).

Earnings-based Index Funds- These type of funds are designed based on earnings prospects and consist of value-based or growth-based companies. Examples are the Vanguard Growth Index Fund (VIGAX) and the Vanguard Value Index Fund (VIVAX).

Term-based Bond Index Funds- Provide fixed income investors with bond terms based on their desired holding period. The funds may be made up of bonds of short-term, intermediate, or long-term maturities. An example is the Vanguard Long-Term Bond Index Fund (VBLAX).

Real Estate Investment Trust Index Funds- This type of fund is designed to track the performance of a specific real estate investment trust. An example of this fund type is the Vanguard Real Estate Index Fund (VGSIX).

Dividend-focused Index Funds- These fund types are designed to provide dividend income. An example of this type of fund is the Vanguard High Dividend Yield Index Fund (VHYAX).

Sector-specific Index Funds- This fund type is designed to track the performance of a specific sector. An example of this fund type is the Vanguard Consumer Discretionary Index Fund (VCDAX).

International Index Funds- This fund type is designed to provide some outside exposure to stocks all over the world. An example is the Vanguard FTSE All World ex-US Index Fund (VFWAX).

Social-responsible Index Funds- These funds invest only in companies that are environmentally friendly, sustainable, or that focus on positive social impact. An example is the Vanguard FTSE Social Index Fund (VFTSX).

Commodity-based Index Funds- This fund type is designed to duplicate the performance of a specific commodity index through the buying and selling of futures. An example is the Vanguard Commodity Strategy Fund (VCMDX).

Remember, what I have listed are just a few of the many different types/sectors of index funds that are available on the stock market. While most can be great wealth builders and can assist with adding diversification to any portfolio, I have found that the best returns are usually the result of keeping things simple. The index investment strategy mentioned earlier is my preference when it comes to creating a powerful, but simple index investing program.

11

POPULAR VANGUARD INDEX FUNDS

Vanguard Total Stock Market Index Fund Admiral Shares (VTSAX)
This fund was created to provide investors with exposure to the entire U.S. equity market and contains a total of 3611 stocks. The top ten holdings make up about 19.4% of the portfolio. This fund has an expense ratio of 0.04% and an average annual return of 13.09% for 10 years as of September 30, 2019.

Vanguard 500 Index Fund Admiral Shares (VFIAX)
This fund provides investors with exposure to 500 of the largest companies in the U.S. The companies contained in this index accounts for about 75% of the U.S. stock market's total value. This fund has an expense ratio of 0.04% and an average annual return of 13.21% for 10 years as of September 30, 2019.

Vanguard Balanced Index Fund Admiral Shares (VBIAX)

This fund contains a mix of stocks and bonds with stocks making up about 60% of the portfolio and bonds accounting for the remaining 40% of the portfolio. This fund has an expense ratio of 0.07% and an average annual return of 9.50% for 10 years as of September 30, 2019.

Vanguard Total Bond Market Index Fund Admiral Shares (VBTLX)

This fund provides wide exposure to U.S. investment grade bonds. This fund invests about 30% in corporate bonds and 70% in U.S. government bonds. This fund contains bonds of all maturities. This fund has an expense ratio of 0.05% and an average annual return of 3.69% for 10 years as of September 30, 2019.

Vanguard Dividend Appreciation Index Fund Admiral Shares (VDADX)

This fund is comprised of high-quality companies that have a history of consistently increasing their dividends with the ability to continue to grow their dividends over the long-term. This fund has an expense ratio of 0.08% and an average annual return of 11.49% for five years as of September 30, 2019.

Vanguard Real Estate Index Fund Admiral Shares (VGSLX)

This fund invests in real estate investment trusts and contains 184 stocks with the 10 largest holdings making up more than 41% of the portfolio's total net assets. This fund has an annual expense ratio of

0.12%, and an average annual return of 12.89% for ten years as of September 30, 2019.

Vanguard Growth Index Fund Admiral Shares (VIGAX)

This fund invests in stocks of large U.S. companies using a buy-and-hold approach. The fund's focus is on growth stocks of companies in sectors that grow faster than the broad market. This fund has an expense ratio of 0.05%, and average annual return of 14.38% for ten years as of September 30, 2019.

12

UNDERSTANDING THE MANAGEMENT EXPENSE RATIO (MER)

T he costs associated with investing in index funds, mutual funds, and exchange-traded funds is probably something that many investors fail to consider before purchasing one of those funds. The truth is that costs should be one of the primary considerations before purchasing any fund.

When it comes to investing in the funds mentioned, the main metric that investors need to check is known as the *management expense ratio (MER),* commonly referred to simply as the expense ratio. In my writings, I will refer to it as the expense ratio since this is the more commonly used reference here in the United States. The expense ratio is a measure of how much of a fund's assets are used for administrative and operating expenses and is calculated annually. Costs such as accounting, record-keeping, legal fees, and other administrative fees make up the expense ratio.

The management expense ratio is given as a percentage of the assets managed or invested by the fund over a year. If you've invested $100,000 in a fund and the management expense ratio is 0.5% per annum, you're paying $500 per annum to retain the fund. The price is subtracted from the return, and the return net of charges, or after taxes, is what you see in your investment report. The expense ratio of management is the management fee plus the administrative costs. The administrative costs typically range from 0.05% to 0.1% of the fund's assets. If the information you obtain refers to a "Management Fee" rather than a "Management Expense Ratio," you would have to add the exact fee to the administrative costs.

For those investors wanting the best investment returns possible, one of the most intelligent things to do is purchase funds with the lowest costs (expense ratio). As I have now mentioned at least a few times in this book, passively managed funds, such as index funds, generally have expense ratios that are much lower than the expense ratios of actively managed funds. Those lower rates are the primary reason that index funds outperform most other funds over the long-term.

Is there a best expense ratio that investors should expect to see based on the type of fund they purchase? The answer is that there isn't a best ratio established, but there are some reasonable ranges established that investors should consider before any purchase. The ratio for passively managed index funds is approximately 0.20%. For actively managed funds 0.50% to 0.75% is the norm. When checking for the expense ratio, it can be found in the fund's prospectus and in reports prepared for the shareholders.

13

TYPES OF MUTUAL FUNDS

Although I'm a firm believer in the superiority of index funds over mutual funds, I realize that the vast majority of funds owned are mutual funds that are offered through employer-sponsored retirement plans such as the 401(k). I also realize that many of those plans tend to be limited in the investment choices they offer and many don't offer index funds. With that being the case, some investors' alternative may only be mutual funds. This is especially true if the employee wants to receive the matching contributions paid into his or her plan by the employer. Those matching contributions are about the only risk-free money an investor can receive. What can be greater than that? So, even though this book is mainly about index funds, I will address the different types of mutual funds here, then in the next section, I will discuss how to invest in them.

The traditional mutual fund is a professionally managed investment fund that pools money from many investors, topurchase securities such as stocks or bonds. In actuality, index funds are considered mutual funds with the difference being that index funds are passively managed.

Investing in mutual funds is done by providing investors with different types of investment options. This falls into the categories broadly: SIP (Systematic Investment Plan), one-time payment, annual, semi-annual, and quarterly payments. SIP was introduced to investors to make regular, equal payments into an account, thereby, taking advantage of *dollar cost averaging*. Therefore, if the security price falls, more shares will be purchased, and fewer shares will be purchased if the securities pricerises.

There are four broad types of mutual funds available on the market. Since the different fund types carry varying degrees of risk and reward potential, an understanding of them is helpful before investing in them. The four broad types are equity funds, bond funds, balanced funds, and money market funds. Other classes or sectors of funds usually fall under one of these four fund types.

Equity Mutual Funds: Also known as stock funds, these funds invest primarily in the stocks of publicly traded companies. Equity mutual funds can be actively or passively managed. This type of fund is riskier than bond funds because it invests only in stocks. The returns will depend on the company's performance in which the fund invests. Nonetheless, on the flip side, because equities have traditionally outperformed all other asset classes, this fund has the highest return potential when compared to the other types.

Bond Funds: Bond funds are fixed-income mutual funds that invest in government and/or corporate debt. Bond funds are available with short, intermediate, or long-term maturities. Generally speaking, bond funds are considered less risky than equity funds.

Money Market Funds: Money market funds are liquid funds. These funds invest in the high-quality debt of corporations, banks, and the government. The goal of the funds is to maintain the principal while yielding a positive return. It is a low-risk investment in return that offers instant liquidity.

Balanced Funds: These funds invests in equity and income-bearing instruments in such a proportion that the portfolio is balanced. The objective is to reduce the risk of investing in stocks by also having an interest in the debt market. It usually yields a reasonable return with moderate exposure to risk. Hybrid funds may be more equity-oriented (60-70% in equity), and debt-oriented hybrid funds may be available (60-70% in debt).

Fund of Funds: Fund of Funds is a secondary fund that invests based on market conditions in different types of funds. For example, if stock markets are in a bearish mood, investing in debt (bonds), rather than equity, may be prudent. Such a fund will, therefore, sell its equity holdings and buy bond fund shares. "Asset allocation funds" is the term used for such funds that take on a macro call and invest in equity, debt, gold, or other security.

Exchange-Traded Funds (ETFs): these are investment funds traded on stock exchanges in the same manner as stocks. You can deal with ETFs intraday, which can't be done with standard funds. In general, these funds are suitable for short-term traders who want to use underlying security to take a position on the market. Based on an article that I read, John Bogle didn't care much for these types of funds. Perhaps, he felt that people would use them as short-term a trading instrument which is one of the primary reasons most investors perform so poorly in the stock market.

14

MUTUAL FUND STRATEGIES

W hy most people invest in mutual funds is easy to understand, but is it a smart play? I would say that the majority of investors choose mutual funds because a) investing in them is a simple process b) some people believe that the professionals should be able to do better than they can when it comes to investing and c) mutual funds are the most commonly offered funds available through the 401(k) plans of most companies. Now, there's nothing you can do about a company that doesn't offer self-directed accounts, but even when presented with that option, most investors would choose the mutual funds route to pick investments for themselves. To further compound the issue, when choosing a mutual fund; most investors select the top performing mutual funds from the previous year and drop it if it begin to perform poorly before repeating the process. Statistics show that over the long-term, this approach won't beat the S&P 500.

There's no doubt that there's plenty of good mutual funds out there; there are some great ones too. The issue is that most investors are not invested in those funds. Why would you put your hard-earned cash into a mutual fund that does not consistently beat the indexes? Why not simply choose an index fund and avoid the fees.

Does anybody like to pay fees? I guess I don't, and you're charged fees for the management of your account. They usually run from 1 to 2 percent, which may not sound like much, but can add up in a hurry. If you started with $100,000 and earned an annual compound rate of return of 4% for 20 years, you would end up with about $210,000 if you paid a low annual fee of 0.25%. If you paid an annual fee of 1% under the same scenario, you would end up with an account value of about $180,000 or about $30,000 less. Just by paying less in fees, you'll have that extra money looking beautiful in your wallet or purse!

If you have a fund that does not perform well, you can bet that the fund manager will probably move in and out of winners and losers owned by the mutual fund. The fund manager will not sit idle and watch stocks that he or she selected put a serious drain on the value of his portfolio. He will feel pressured to react and will react with buy and sell transactions. Buy and sell transactions are music to the ears of the brokerages that maintain the accounts. For every stock that is bought or sold, they collect transaction fees. Who do you think will pay for it?

Strategiesforbettermutualfundperformance:

- Start investing as early as possible. It is very possible for an individual who invests a specific amount into a retirement account from the age of 20 to 30 to end up with a larger nest egg than the individual that begins at age 30, and contributes until the age of 65 if both contributed the same amount annually and earned the same annualized returns.

- Identify your goals. Are you looking for current income or would you prefer long-term capital appreciation? When do you want to achieve your goals? How much risk are you willing to take? These are the types of questions that you must ask yourself, to determine which types of mutual funds you need to be invested in.

- Invest consistently. To make money with mutual funds, you must invest consistently into those funds for the long-term. Do not constantly switch your money from one fund to another, because doing so will more than likely lead to poor performance.

- Look for funds that have been steady, consistent performers over the long haul. Try to identify funds that have been consistent for the most recent five or ten year period.

- Pay attention to a mutual fund's expense ratio. As with index funds, the expense ratio is very important with mutual funds too. With mutual funds, an expense ratio above 1% is considered very high. The lower the expense ratio, the better when it comes to all fund types.

- Look for a low turnover ratio. Index funds tend to have almost zero turnovers. Because mutual funds are actively managed, depending on the funds objective, their turnover ratio can get very high. Mutual funds with turnover ratios below 50% are the better bargains.

- See if the fund's management has been at the helm for a long time. Look for management that has been in place and managing the fund for a minimal of five years. Of course, the longer, the better.

- When evaluating the performance of funds, compare apples to apples. This may or may not be possible if you are investing through a retirement plan that contains a very limited selection of mutual funds in it.

- Diversify. Divide your money between three to four different types of mutual funds. This is a recommendation made by Peter Lynch in his book titled *Beating the Street.*

JAMES PATT ERSENN JR

60 | JAMES PATT ERSENN JR

15

EXCHANGE-TRADED FUNDS (ETFS)

As an option to addressing retirement or risk-based mutual funds, many 401(k) open architecture providers enable retirement plan advisors to create their own managed models for inclusion in the investment menu of a plan. One of the reasons for this is the ability to create an asset allocation plan that uses multiple investment managers' investments. A number of these advisor-managed models often include an aspect of passive investment, i.e., index fund. In their relatively low cost, the appeal of these' passively managed' offers— is in their ability to consistently produce market-like returns.

Although retirement plan advisors have traditionally had only the option to use index mutual funds as the passive portion of their controlled models, most retirement plan providers have recently made available exchange-traded funds (ETFs) for inclusion in the investment lineup of a 401(k) program. Passively managed ETFs, like index mutual funds, passively follow their benchmark and have low expense ratios.

One of the significant differences between ETFs and index mutual funds is that ETFs can be traded intraday like stocks. Most retirement plan sites, however, offer only once a day priced ETFs. We deal in precisely the same way as mutual funds in this respect. The primary benefit, though, would tend to be its lower expense ratio to choose an ETF over an index mutual fund in a retirement plan. But while one could presume that all things being equal, the option with the lower expense ratio would be the best investment choice. All items are not the same in this case. We cannot forget that an ETF is likely to charge a commission for both the purchase and the sale of the ETF in a retirement plan, whereas most index mutual funds are "no charge" and do not charge a purchase commission. That doesn't mean that the ETF may not be the best choice— it could very well be depending on the model's investment management approach of the advisor.

If you are deciding whether an ETF or alternative mutual fund is better suited to your controlled models, you should consider the following:

ETF commissions paid by the program provider: an investment of $1000 in an index mutual fund would result in a balance of $1000. However, if your plan provider charges a commission to purchase an ETF, a purchase of $1000 will result in a balance of less than $1000 as the commission amount will reduce the proceeds amount. A corresponding selling fee will also be in place to sell the ETF.

ETF share price: If the records keeper of your open architecture 401(k) plan pays a premium to buy and sell an ETF, the higher share value ETF will result in lower commission charges. For example, assume that you are buying two S&P 500 ETFs with the same expense ratios, you are seeking to buy $1000 worth of each ETFs for your portfolio, and your retirement plan provider charges $0.05 per share fee. If one of the ETFs trades at $100 and the other trades at $50, the commission sum will double for the $50 per ETF share as you buy twice as many shares. While a mutual fund's share price is seldom a consideration used to determine an alternative, the same cannot be said for an ETF.

Expenditure ratios for both products: Given that the ETF has a lower expense ratio but also pays a fee, you may have to keep the ETF for a more extended period of superior performance (due to the lower expense ratio) to compensate for the purchase and sale commissions. The period would benefit directly from how much smaller the ETF's expense ratio is than the benchmark mutual fund's. The ability to include either ETFs or index mutual funds in the core investment lineup of the plan or within a managed model is one of the main benefits of using an open architecture 401(k) plan provider.

16

TRACKING ERROR AND OTHER INVESTMENT TERMINOLOGY EXPLAINED

Since each fund has costs to run it, you're not going to get the benchmark 100 percent of the time, because that means you're going to invest for free. The tracking error is the difference between the benchmark's measured return and the actual return provided by the passive fund or portfolio imitating a benchmark fund. For example, if the S&P 500 index had a gain of 5% for a one year period and 10% for two years, and the fund had a return of 4.5% for the one year period and 9.5% for two years, then the tracking error would be 0.5% each year.

Tracking error tends to be reasonably consistent overall, but not entirely consistent as the cost of running a fund will vary; and sometimes the act of trying to follow an index can become tricky if that index is very volatile or illiquid. The tracking error is not a fee per se, but it is a way to measure the cost of owning the real fund versus the index that it's compared to. Tracking error is also useful in determining how consistently, from a cost perspective, the fund is managed.

Early Redemption Fee

If you sell your fund within a short time, some companies charge an early redemption fee. It will depend on the institution and how short the period is. It may be 30 days in some cases, but it may be 90 days, six months, one year, or some other period. This fee is intended to discourage the product from rapid redemption that results from short-term trading.

Selling Loads

Sales fees/loads for passive funds would only refer to a fund that is sold through a salesperson. In most situations, you can get the same fund without the salesperson. Passive funds generally have no sales charges, but the exception would be if a consultant recommends the funds and charge you a fee. This would be another question to ask if you are advised to purchase a passive fund and don't see any direct costs to purchase the product.

Account Administrative Fees

Some institutions charge administrative fees to transfer securities to or from your account, or an annual administrative fee to keep your account open. These fees may depend on how much money you have with the institution, and may be reduced or waived as the balance of your account increases. These fees tend to be a flat amount rather than a percentage, which means that they are relatively small compared to the assets that the account may contain.

Trading fees

Typically, these fees will be a flat fee per trade, depending on how often you trade and what kind of investment you trade. Generally speaking, the more often you trade, and the more exotic the product you trade, the higher the cost.

Foreign exchange fees

Each time you swap money, foreign exchange conversion charges must occur. This could be for withdrawals, securities exchanges, or re-balancing among securities or funds denominated in other currencies. The currency exchange rate, most of the time, has to do with the U.S. dollar, but if you have foreign accounts or spend passively, it may be in another currency.

Bid Request Spreads and Opportunity Costs

Spreads refers to the bid and request for the price of a given security. You always pay the "ask" price or the higher price the seller wants to receive when you buy something, and you would receive the "bid" price or the lower price the buyer wants to receive when you sell something. The difference is called the spread between them. Consider a price quote for the fund you wish to buy when the market is open, and you will see the bid-ask spread when you look at any quote for the fund to know how much this would be. The difference between the value of the bid and the cost of the offer would be the dollar amount you pay. This difference divided by the fund's purchase price would be the percentage cost. For instance, if a fund has an $8.00 bid price and an $8.10 ask price, you'd pay 10 cents per unit or share as a spread. If you purchased the fund at $8.10, it would cost $0.10/$8.10 or 1.2%. This percentage is a one-time fee for each pair of trades to buy and sell. The longer you keep your investment, and if the price increases as expected, the cheaper this spread will be in percentages, as the investment value tends to rise over time. If the value goes down for a given investment, the reverse would happen. Over time, the spread can vary depending on how much volume trades at a particular time of day.

If you decide to set the price for buying or selling security instead of going in at the prevailing price at the moment or "the market," you run the risk of not receiving the protection or paying much more for it at a later date. This is called the cost of opportunity, and with each trade, it will differ a bit, but it does exist.

AdvisoryCharges

Separate advisory charges apply to a situation where you would pay for advice and the services you are purchasing separately. This would be important if you are paying a commission for the financial service manager, a financial planner, money coach, or consultant who charges a flat fee for advice separately from any items you invest in.

17

WHATIFI'DLIKETODOITALONE?

That's one of the stock market's beauties; no one can tell you that you, as an individual, aren't supposed to invest in the stock market. But if you're planning to succeed, especially when it comes to investing in individual stocks, it takes a serious commitment. Winning in the stock market requires an understanding of stock market investment fundamentals, a clear investment plan, and good resources.

The first thing you need to do is start learning. You can start by reading *The Intelligent Investor,* written by Benjamin Graham, and then read about Warren Buffett and his investment strategies and methodology. Both of these people are giants in the investment world, and their views deserve a certain level of respect because of their amazing success. In addition, you can read my first book titled, *You Can Invest Like a Stock Market Pro*. Your learning should also include a growing understanding of Wall Street's stock market terms and techniques.

Next, you need to develop an investment plan. Identify your goals and a course to get you there. Make your plans as appropriate. What type of stocks do you desire to invest in? Will they be growth stocks or value stocks or both? Do you prefer the idea of trading futures markets or options? What are your strategies to reduce risk? Understanding these things will allow you to create a plan that will increase your chances of success.

When investing in stocks or the stock market, simplicity has always proven to be a vital component when it comes to the best and safest investment strategies for building wealth. The assumption is that nothing beats index funds for the average investor. Index funds are a simple, secure way for the average or small investor to invest and prosper. Index funds allow the small investor to relax, realizing he or she is using the stock market's most consistently performing investment tool. Index funds have become a major force in the investing world. As late as 2016, more than $1 out of every $5 invested in the equity markets here in the United States, is invested in index funds.

18

CONCLUSION

P assive investment has the same setup as active investment, but the portfolio manager would copy a benchmark instead of deciding what securities to buy or how much to buy. A benchmark is a securities collection compared to the fund to see how well it does. Since it's all, every fund out there is trying to compare all the other same type of funds, to see who can make the most money. The benchmark is the basis for comparisons, and then it becomes a comparison between peers or similarly managed funds. Comparisons are only made for returns in general. The risk part of the equation is approached by looking at what kind of assets the fund owns or how the fund is qualified. How do I know by the name of the fund if it is activeorpassive?

The simple answer is you need to know how the fund manager is running the fund. Some clues are given to find out faster if the fund is active or passive next. This is active management if they intentionally try to pick securities according to some of the beliefs they have about the market. If the description of the fund speaks of "manager skill," or "beating the benchmark" then it is managed actively. Another indication is to look at the history of the return. If returns vary by different amounts each year compared to the index, the fund will be actively managed. Last but not least, the fees may be costly and have loads of sales.

If the fund name says "Index" or "Index Fund," there is also a good chance the fund will be managed passively. If the fund's name says "ETF," this may be a passive fund, but you need to make sure that this is because some ETFs are actually active funds, but they are managed in some way. Claymore, BMO, iShares, Horizons, Vanguard, and others provide most of the passively managed ETFs where the holdings are from the United States. Most of the other businesses would only have managed fundsactively.

If the description of the fund states that the fund attempts to "imitate" an index or benchmark's performance, this implies that it copies the index and that it is managed passively. From the point of view of return, passively managed funds will be very close to the index they claim to imitate, but slightly less each year due to fees. Every year, the amount that the returns are under the index will be nearly identical unless there is currency conversion or cost variance that may result from currency hedging or fluctuations that the fund can do. Typically, passive funds do not have loads of sales as they are aimed at people who invest forthemselves.

There are some funds that attempt to combine active and passive management. Such funds can be considered to be actively managed, but their returns will be closer to the benchmark than most other funds, so if the deviation from the index is a variable, this is something to consider.

Thank you so much for reading this book!

If you have enjoyed this book and have a minute to spare, I would appreciate a short review on the page or website from which you bought the book. Even if you didn't like it, I would appreciate your feedback.

Reviews can be tough to come by these days. You, the reader, have the power to make or break a book. I would certainly appreciate it if you would go to the appropriate link provided below and complete a short review of this work.

In gratitude,

James Pattersenn Jr.

AmazonLink:
https://www.amazon.com/review/create-review/listing

Goodreads Link:
https://www.goodreads.com/review/new/49754389-common-sense-investing-with-index-funds

Barnes & Noble Link:
https://www.barnesandnoble.com/w/common-sense-investing-with-index-funds-james-pattersenn-jr/1137201715?ean=2940162694663

Google Play Link:
https://play.google.com/store/books/details?id=fbjrDwAAQBAJ

KoboLink:
https://www.kobo.com/us/en/ebook/common-sense-investing-with-index-funds

Your Free Gift

As a way of showing my appreciation, I want to send you my FREE REPORT,

5 Highly-Rated ETFs That Can Make You Rich.

Contained within this report are:

- ETFs that have easily outperformed the overall stock market over the last decade and beyond!
- ETFs that are highly-rated by professional investment analysts!
- ETFs that offer high return opportunities and are excellent long-term plays!
- ETFs that hold some of the best and most financially sound companies in the world.
- ETFs that are predicted to deliver big returns well beyond the pandemic!

Please enter your email at the link below and I will send you a copy of this Free Report:

https://mailchi.mp/30fb211f84c6/common-sense-investing-with-index-funds

Other books by the author

You Can Invest Like A Stock Market Pro:

How to Use Simple and Powerful Strategies of the World's Greatest Investors to Build Wealth

https://www.amazon.com/dp/B07G9PW4F2

Now That You Can Invest Like a Pro:

More Principles and Strategies for Building Wealth

Like the World's Greatest Investors

https://www.amazon.com/dp/B07ZJMV7ZK

Common Sense Investing With Stock Screeners

The Intelligent Investor's Guide to Using

Free Online Stock Screeners to Find Winning Stocks

https://www.amazon.com/dp/B08DQM4SQZ

100 Stocks That a Young Warren Buffett Might Buy:

If He Invested Like He Does Today

https://www.amazon.com/dp/B07T7XFQNW

Acknowledgments

Mysincerethanksto:

Carrie Pattersenn, my sweet and unselfish mother. She taught me the importance of putting the needs of others before my own if I truly wanted to be blessed and to be a blessing.

The great investors who have made this book possible because they cared enough to willingly share their wisdom and knowledge about investing with the rest ofus.

Angie, a professional graphic designer, whom I found at Fiverr (the world's largest freelance services marketplace). She does amazing work, and you are going to love her prices! If you need an eBook cover or printed book cover, hire her. She can be contacted at https://www.fiverr.com/inbox/pro_ebookcovers

Timason, a professional graphic artist and engineer, whom I discovered at Fiverr. I'm always very happy with the excellent job that he does formatting my books. He does high-quality work at such affordable prices. I will continue to hire him for all of my future projects. He can be found on Fiverr where he has been a member for more than five years with a perfect 5-Star rating! He can be contacted at https://www.fiverr.com/inbox/tlmason

Proof Royalty, a professional proofreading service that does an excellent job of improving my writing to make me look smarter than I really am! Proof Royalty can be contacted at https://www.fiverr.com/inbox/proof_royalty

Most of all, I thank God, the Father, and my Lord Jesus Christ, who is gracious and merciful to all.

If you have any questions, comments, or suggestions, I would love to hear from you. I can be contacted at:

trilogypublishinggroup@gmail.com

Made in the USA
Las Vegas, NV
03 October 2023

78522686R00046